The Little Old Art of Love

Armand Silvestre and Cor Charron

Published by Cor Charron, 2024.

While every precaution has been taken in the preparation of this book, the publisher assumes no responsibility for errors or omissions, or for damages resulting from the use of the information contained herein.

THE LITTLE OLD ART OF LOVE

First edition. January 1, 2024.

Copyright © 2024 Armand Silvestre and Cor Charron.

ISBN: 979-8223992691

Written by Armand Silvestre and Cor Charron.

The Little Art of Love.

Armand Silvestre

Chapter One : Of the Choice of a Lover

I

It's not the first time that one of the kind individuals who graciously consult me on matters of amorous aesthetics confesses to finding solitude burdensome and expresses a desire for a lover. There was a time when I would have had an immediate response to such a letter, without even needing to dip my pen into the inkwell. Today, I no longer have the conceit to believe that a purely theatrical response is sought from me, and that it's simply a matter of initiating a connection. This is an idea that wouldn't occur to a sensibly minded young lady. I no longer go to the city after having been there a lot—not enough yet, as the best times of life are those spent in these heartful retreats. Back then, I only wrote when I was tired of my visits. Love was the play, and literature was merely the intermissions. I confined myself, as a writer, to compiling the verses I had composed for my good friends into volumes. Now, literature is the play, and love is the intermissions. My spectacle in an armchair—and even on a sofa—has suffered greatly. But why should I complain? I still love the woman with the same passion, albeit without proving it with the same eloquence. Despite putting stones in my mouth, like Demosthenes, it is certain that my pronunciation deficiency worsens day by day. But I do not yet stutter. At most, I may lisp a little. It really isn't worth exposing myself to swallowing stones.

Therefore, now, it is without seeking personal gain that I respond, as seriously as a candidate being criticized, to questions of the kind posed to me today, with a frankness I want to acknowledge above all. You don't beat around the bush, Madam. You confess that you find your bed too wide and that you want a companion in it. It is both clear and insightful. But you ask me how to choose this companion, and that is not as easy as you seem to believe. I agree, however, that your case is one of the simplest in the world, as you are the only one interested in this delicate adventure, and you don't have to satisfy the tastes of a husband at the same time as your own, which sometimes makes things difficult.

Because couples rarely agree in this matter on a common ideal. Some men insist on being made cuckolds in certain rituals and in a certain way, that is, only by people who suit them, which is only fair—who, for example, play whist or dominoes with them every evening, or take them to the theater for free, or give them some money for their small pleasures and outings. But let's set aside these sybarites or the tactless and focus only on you, Madam. You are free, you say, and I really cannot congratulate you enough on that. It's an adorable condition for forging pleasant chains. Because Freedom, which politicians want to make a force, is simply a milieu, like Faith, which is only a fact, and which Christians want to make a virtue. It's the breathable air and the open space before our movements, that's all. It's the viable atmosphere of caprice and fancy, the only goods we have in the world. Freedom is that form of wisdom that allows us to make a mistake. I will assist you to the best of my ability, oh free and trusting creature.

II

Firstly, learn, Madam, if you do not already know, that from the perspective of Love, men can be classified into two categories—not those who pay for it and those who do not, for I want to leave aside the commercial viewpoint—but those for whom Love is the only thing in life, the _summum omnino bonum_ of the monk A. Kempis (excuse me, Madam, for this saintly Latin, but I hope you are not a freethinker), and those for whom it is merely a pleasant distraction, a pastime like bingo and billiards. Des Grieux, if you will, on one side; and Emperor Napoleon, on the other, who made it a simple interlude between two victories. Both were deceived, but Des Grieux was at least loved, which is indeed a consolation... I don't need to tell you that the second category, that of the conqueror of Austerlitz, doesn't even deserve your attention; because your desire does not seem to be precisely to become an empress. It's not the throne of the West that you're thinking of, but your bed, on which we have much more chance of meeting, by the way. Because, like me, you do not hold the eagle and the crown in high esteem, and prefer a hundred kisses from such lips that I know well. So, let's recognize the chosen ones who make up the first class, the only ones that my conscience allows me to recommend to you. Let's enumerate the signs of their race.

Firstly, in terms of physical appearance. Well, it will be a certain casual air that, if I didn't warn you against yourself, would first deter your refined inclinations and naturally delicate tastes against them.

Someone who truly loves a woman and loves her exclusively— the only way to love her—never concerns himself with being handsome. It is perfectly illogical on his part, as he thus loses a means of pleasing a heap of little ladies and charming creatures that he is ready to find witty: but that's how it is.

Self-denial is at the core of all sincere worship. For those who are truly captivated by a woman's beauty, everything in the world disappears before her, and even themselves on top of that. Their ideal is higher than them, purely objective, and they only wish to be living dust on the path their adored steps tread. You can trust me, Madam: the gentleman, otherwise charming and benevolent, who has spent four hours on his toilette before appearing before you, is not your type. But the dishonest one who hasn't done it at all is not either. Because if the inner contemplation of his beauty does not allow, for the perfect lover I wish for you, to look at himself, respect forbids him to appear before her in an outfit that horrifies her. Well-organized women are, above all, beings of moderation—I won't say the same for men!—Show your insight in this matter, Madam, and also your moderation, by taking and leaving what I tell you.

III

Let's now turn to the moral aspect, if you please.

Here, for instance, I have my absolute sentiment, and I give you, as certain, my diagnosis. Love has only one serious enemy here below: self-love. It is against it that you must direct all the trials to which you subject the neophyte before admitting him into the temple (I believe the image is nobly turned), or uttering the ***"Dignus, dignus es intrare!"*** of the comedy, to quote Molière aptly. Propose to him, boldly, to obtain from you a favor—oh! my God, the slightest one!—a favor as significant as your little finger, the smallest of favors! a flower, for example, fallen from your bodice and bruised by your pretty foot. Propose to him, I say, to perform an act of overwhelming stupidity that would make him grotesque in the eyes of the entire universe. If he hesitates for a single moment, kick him out the door. There are those who do not hesitate every day, and they are the true lovers!

All of this is for the serious side of the benefits you expect from him. But do not neglect the more purely amiable aspects of the matter. Guard yourself preciously from a jealous lover. Contrary to popular opinion, it is not Love that jealousy proves, but its most relentless enemy, Self-love. It's a characteristic of selfish and stingy temperaments. I have seen women seriously jealous of their husbands who were deceiving them during the day—because it's only lovers who are deceived at night—due to this monstrous feeling, quite common among women, that everything is owed to them and that they owe nothing to the rest of humanity, not even excuses for having us expelled from Paradise! But there are also men of this ilk. They must be avoided like the plague. Take a kind, gentle, and trusting soul who does not believe that the Infinite is divisible and who is quite right. Because all of us can say to the woman we have loved, with the poet:

What I loved in you was my own intoxication!

And this intoxication, all the infidelities in the world cannot steal from us. To the one to whom you give, Madam, the immense joy of Love, who could boast of stealing something from it, since this happiness is made of impressions that are absolutely personal to him, and the woman is like an instrument from which everyone draws the air that pleases them?

Similarly, do not choose a glutton or a jealous person as your lover. Good food is also an enemy of Love. Passionate strength belongs to the temperate and moderate. It is an old foolishness accredited by songs that Bacchus and Venus make a good match. The lover with some fervor wants to apply himself entirely to the conscious possession of the beloved mistress; between her and him, he does not want vain smoke, but only the incense that burns in his heart to rise towards her.

But above all, Madam, do not take a politician as a lover either. You would return to me so cruelly disenchanted within eight days that I would have to get back to work, and frankly, I cannot spend all my time furnishing your bed. A politician, poor woman! God save you from this unpleasant creature particular to the times we live in, from this buzzing cockchafer that doesn't even have the mitigating circumstance of being of a single season. Preserve, for the resonant bees of the kiss, your blossoming flowers and good luck now!

Chapter Two : WHO LOVE THE MOST

I

I would need to quote the entire letter that inspires this new commentary on the only subject that has interested me in life to answer it properly. In any case, the reader wouldn't lose anything, as, as you will be able to judge by a few passages, it is in a distinctly French form—clear and elegant, very precise in its questions. The writer engages in a dialogue with her lover about the subtleties of love borrowed from their own tenderness. I am somewhat skeptical about a passion that philosophizes. The question at hand is determining who loves the other more. I'll tell you right away, Mademoiselle. It's the one who, first, interrupts this discussion by closing his lips on the lips of his interlocutor and embracing him with his arms. The true and only language of Love is the kiss. Those who are truly in love are anything but talkative. The necessary weariness imposed by possession is occupied by true lovers through silent contemplations and silent adorations rather than pretty speeches. The one of you two who loves the most is the one who withdraws first from these useless conversations.

I quote now: "He tells me: you accuse me of loving less than you because I show you the dangers of our secret liaison, dangers that I despise through love, but that I know and measure... Is the young soldier, ignorant of danger, who rushes into battle, as deserving as the old veteran who walks into the fire, knowing well that wounds are received there and that one sometimes dies? I also know that the most ardent loves have the fragility of all earthly things, and a day will inevitably come when we will cherish less. To this I respond: My love is greater because it prevents me from seeing the danger; I do not want to know it and avert my eyes when you try to make me perceive its dark specter, and the cruel thought of an end never haunting my dreams painfully."

You could have replied to him, Mademoiselle: "I love you more because the danger you mention, and that we both bravely face, exists, in reality, only for me." When a secret liaison is discovered, a man may lose some of his peace of mind; but the young girl certainly loses her honor and the respect for her entire life. The game is truly not equal, and a gentleman talking about his personal risks in such a situation is somewhat laughable. Unless he is of such conscience and internal honesty that the greatest misfortune he fears is compromising a destiny other than his own. But those are rare, and they have also taken precautions to not decline any responsibility and to sacrifice themselves if necessary. Because actions are indifferent in intimate morality, and the only crime, vis-à-vis ourselves, is the cowardice that avoids the foreseen consequences. There is nothing to say to a man who, seducing a girl, is determined to marry her without any ulterior motive; who, fathering a child, is ready to raise it; who, killing, is ready to die himself.

The argument of your admirer touches me more when he speaks of the courage it takes to love again when one has loved before, that is to say, measured the great open abysses that love leaves behind, counted the tears it costs, and the great stripping away of illusions that it carries away like a storm. But that is only specious. Because if he has learned that love is not an eternal thing, he also knows that love is the only thing worth braving everything for, and without which living is no longer possible when one has loved. So, the great merit of facing it again when one could no longer do without it! It's like a man who would think himself heroic because he breathes, even though the air sometimes gives us chest colds!

After having suffered, one must suffer again.

One must love again after having loved!

exclaimed one of the poets who have suffered the most and the worst from Love. So submit to the inexorable fate that you know, without taking on airs of bravado, oh you who know well that you cannot escape the battle where you are already defeated in advance! Do not compare yourself to the boiling Ajax to rush again into a melee where arrows are at the rosy tips of bare breasts and wounds are in the purple of swooning lips. I'll make you a hero at that price! You are the one who is right, Mademoiselle, and even the man, often disappointed, truly loves only when he has forgotten his own experience, imagines that this time it will last forever, that everything he has lived was only the preludes of his life, and believes he loves naively for the first time. Ah! That one truly loves more than the less knowledgeable mistress, whose merit is less great for not remembering. But that is not the case with your admirer, since he doubts.

II

I continue to quote: "You reproach me for loving less than you, my lover says again, because I struggle in the bonds that ensnare me more and more; which gradually, from the caprice of the beginning, make a deep sentiment where all my heart is taken, where my reason will be lost... I had sworn to always escape a powerful love, and here I am wearing chains that I should break and from which I cannot and do not want, alas! free myself. You can see that it is I who love the most and the best, since, in wanting to forget you, I adore you even more!—Isn't it so, I say in turn, to love less already than to feel the slavery of our love? Is not my tenderness stronger, since its chains do not weigh on me, and the narrow prison in which I have voluntarily confined myself seems like a paradise from which I never want to be expelled!"

I will respond to you, Mademoiselle, with a small piece of bad Latin taken from a book you may have read occasionally during your virginal purity, the "Imitation of Christ." *It says: _Magna res est amor, magnum omnino bonum quod leve facit omne onerosum. Nam onus sine onere portat._* I translate: Love is a great thing, the greatest of all; for it makes light everything that is heavy and does not feel the weight of burdens. I confess that this text is absolutely in your favor. And yet you are not entirely right. A little ungentlemanly, even a bit cynical in my opinion, your lover confesses to you that you were, at the beginning, just a whim for him. It wasn't enough for you to yield to him, Mademoiselle, if you cared about your virtue. One does not embark on a secret and, it seems, dangerous liaison for so little. I'm sure you deserved more and would have certainly found it. Anyway, this brave lad has the honesty, otherwise perfectly useless, to tell you, and that he only intended to compromise you for a simple affair of the heart. In that case, it is highly illogical to tell him that he already loves less because he feels his enslavement. On the contrary, he is only beginning to love, and he will only forget it on the day when he loves even more. As for the oath he made to himself to always avoid true love, he is a man much less wise in life than he thinks he is. I can even assure you that he understands nothing and knows much less than you do. Without this ignorance, he would have realized that, in the world of passion, we do not escape anything at all, that everything there is fate, and swearing not to love again is to make even the drunks laugh who know the emptiness of such words. We do not love when we want to; and that's your excuse, you who seem to have loved a little too lightly. It's a law that we endure and that would be wrong to accuse. Because it is sweet. You are wrong, Sir, to want to "break your chains." Those that the white arms of women knot around ours are the best thing I know in life, and the invisible net, with which their hair entwines us, makes a slow and subtle caress of this delightful imprisonment.

III

I quote again: "And, to conclude, which sentiment has more value? His love, with all its ardor, but his reasonings, his little touch of deliberate skepticism, that experience gives... or mine, with infinite abandon, the blind and grateful tenderness of a first love that, from the cold young girl of yesterday, has made today the woman with a heart vibrating with deliciously new and unknown sensations?" One must be a tough goldsmith, Mademoiselle, to measure the title of a sentiment and appreciate its "value." I believe, however, that our feelings are worth more as selfishness is more foreign to them and as a greater part of sacrifice is involved. The morality of actions has always seemed to me to be defined by the ratio between what they give us of satisfaction and what they sacrifice to an ideal higher than ourselves. Which of you two brings more selflessness into your tenderness? That is what should be known to answer you. Currently, both of you find it to your advantage. You, a girl from yesterday, savoring the intoxication of "deliciously new and unknown sensations." You, a young man of yesteryear, comically exuding the complaints of a martyr from whom you would not, for anything in the world, want to be relieved. For charming instruments of torture are a pink and fresh mouth that kisses you, an unfolding of ingenuous tenderness that embraces you, a blossoming of caresses that opens only for you and opens heaven to you. Those who are tortured in this way are more envied than pitied, and you have chosen a kind of intermittent death that does great credit to your taste. As long as you are in this exchange of enchantments, I will not tell you what your love is worth, to both of you. I am waiting for some obstacle to put your two hearts to the test. Then I will know the weight of this skepticism, perhaps false, and what this gratitude, currently all sensual, has of enduring. You are still in the game of love. Its great battle awaits you, where souls are truly measured. The dangers that one braves with some puerile ostentation, that the other forgets, perhaps more by childishness than by passion, will become realities. The one who loves the most is the one who will bring to the struggle the most courage and, above all, selflessness, the one who will be faithful to pain as well as to joy, the one who will be happy to suffer rather than forget!

Chapter Three: What is Meant by the Heart

18

I

The cherubs, in their poses, reveal to us
    What Boufflers calls the heart,
    sings a song more than light. It is certainly not that one
    you are referring to, Madam, you who write me a letter
    of which I marvelously understand the sentiment, but whose
expressions,
    somewhat troubling in their vagueness, make my response difficult.
    It is clear that you pity me for my excessively plastic concerns
    in love, and would like me to incorporate some moral elements.
    I believe you think that esteem is necessary in love.
    Baudelaire would have replied, with his genius brutality:
    Cursed be forever the useless dreamer
    Who wanted, the first, in his stupidity,
    Falling in love with an insoluble and sterile problem,
    To mix honesty with matters of love!
    You rightly add that you only want to hear about "true love."
    I would appreciate it if you could tell me what the other is.
    Is the love that causes suffering, the love that leads to death, true?
    Do you believe that Antoine's love for Cleopatra, or Des Grieux's
love
    for Manon—because characters from history and novels are alike
    in the face of passionate synthesis—were true loves?
    It doesn't seem to me that they were precisely based on esteem.
    You also clearly reproach me for "considering" Beauty always "from
the same angle."
    In love, Beauty, like Truth, seems to me not subject to any
misunderstanding.
    It either is or it isn't. I will concede to you that it can sometimes be
    in the countenance as much as in the regularity of features.
    But only for a few chosen ones. And then, the countenance itself,

which you consider a faithful mirror of the Soul, can be deceptive.
I maintain that the safest thing is the plastic harmony of forms and
faces,
the splendor of flesh, the opulence of hair, the beautiful design of
lips
and throat—things that are not prone to deceit. The gaze and the
smile
can be deceiving, but not the color of the eyes and the curve of the
mouth.
However, it is understood that you seek, for love, beyond Beauty.
I find you demanding, and I wonder where you find this beyond.
Because Beauty seems to me the last word, the supreme reason for
everything that exists.
What you need is "the heart."
Here is the word that worries me. In love, I see no other definition
than the one I gave you earlier. The "heart" is what causes suffering.
Now, the choice in us of this divine suffering is not free,
and we do not have to delve into its fatalism.
You would make narrow and petty the great passion law
that governs humanity since the origin of souls,
restricting it to voluntary selections, lowering it to the scruples of
reason
and the revolts of conscience! You would truly take away from it
everything that is divine and mysterious, and we, the true lovers,
would reject this suffering that would not come from higher than
us,
from the very top of the altars where pagan incenses still smoke,
still red from the blood of human victims at the feet
of the immortal specter of the unique Beauty! Ah! Let us, at least,
keep the painful grandeur of the most sublime of these dreams,
we who seek in caresses only the delights of annihilation.

II

You say again: the woman who is only beautiful... Only! It's
   cruel to say, but only she has a reason to exist, even from
   the perspective of the dignity of races, in reproduction. It would be
   necessary for all mothers to be beautiful so that humanity does not
   decline! Their womb should not be just a furrow where the
   seed germinates, but an august mold where the brain takes its
imprint,
   where muscles are shaped for the rugged tasks of life. You
   see, therefore, that one is virtuous and wise who seeks noble
physical
   beauty in a woman. Do not ask another cause for the prestige of
love
   marriages, in the obscure conscience but sagacious depths of the
masses,
   and the disdain, insufficient in my opinion, that attaches to money
marriages.
   For those are wrongdoers who scatter abortions into the world,
   even dressed in silk and velvet. They spit into the sources of life
   where all the forces of the future come to drink. To love a woman
for her beauty is the
   first of duties, Madam. Love that attaches to plastic splendors is
simply the savior of the human stock
   and delays its degeneration. Ah! You are generous in admitting that
"only a
   beautiful woman can inspire Passion"! But you are wrong to add
that she cannot inspire true Love,
   and to corroborate this monstrosity with the following comment:
"That's why women with heart do not give themselves,
   fearing to be loved only for fragile charms subject to fading with
age."

Oh! Madam, how I find that true morality is on my side!

Under the pretext that your charms are fragile, you deny

the joy of them to the one who loves you, and because they will fade, you deem

it useless to use them in their bloom. You are, at the same time, selfish

towards others and cruel to yourself. Is it madness to breathe in the fragrance of the rose today

because it will be just a withering tomorrow, and do you not know the delicious perfume

that faded roses still retain? Thus, for those who have loved you, oh women, in

the bloom of your youth and beauty, a subtle aroma of your departed charms

remains a very sweet blindness where your wrinkles fade, where your lips regain

the carmine that was kissed for a long time in the past! Memory is a magician whose power

and ingenious lies you are unaware of. But, even apart from past lovers,

for the lovers of others who pass by only, but who have

similar fervors in their hearts, the woman who has truly been beautiful

retains an indelible prestige, a glorious stigma before which

all respects kneel. I dare say that a woman who has

truly been beautiful always is. It is even by this that true beauty is measured.

So do not be so sparing, Madam, of what does not

wear out as much as you think. You are ignorant of the essence

of love if you do not know that it lies in abandonment, in

the constant sacrifice of one's entire being, in the desire to utterly lose oneself in a more beautiful being, in the living ideal that Beauty presents

before us! A woman who truly loves always fears, contrary to you, not giving herself enough. She would want to be even more beautiful to give more, more and forever. For it is not love to save oneself for other loves.

III

Ah, the heart. This heart you talk about so much; this heart that you need,

    for the true love you desire, but it is made of those torments

    that you repel with an impious concern for your tranquility. It is

    made of those terrors and despairs in the face of irremediable human nothingness,

    but also of the joyful courage with which one savors them and defies them.

    It is made of the beats that fill our chest with the approach of the beloved or

    the lover, and the blood that lifts it, in tumultuous rhythms,

    is the blood we would want to redden the divine feet of Beauty.

    Those have truly loved who have loved in this way, in the dream of a very gentle death

    because it warmed, so to speak, another life and the last breath of it was

    sipped by beloved lips. If you have not been jealous of what dies for the one you love,

    you do not know of what desperate, monstrous, and mad desires true love is made,

    the one under which plastic splendor crushes us, envious of the insect that a woman's foot crushes in the sand!

    The senses! You call that: the senses! But find me other

    means of living, that is, of loving, than by and for them! We

    are dupes in this of the coarseness of methods that only recognize five,

    when everything today proves that we possess an infinite number of absolutely subtle ones,

    defying time and space. It is of those that our heart movements undoubtedly speak.

For there is a certain immateriality of matter undeniable now. But let's stay in the realm of

pure philosophy, the one that the examples of other men and our own torments teach us.

You lower love, Madam, by thinking to elevate it with I don't know what concerns of esteem and morality.

It is far above our human proprieties and yet is capable

of an honesty higher than all others: that by which one gives oneself entirely and withholds nothing of oneself.

Its greatness lies in the absolute nature of this surrender, in this sublime self-denial

of all interests, in this merciless sacrifice. It was the law

of the most glorious lovers, and it will be the law of all future lovers

worthy of the name. But do not seek elsewhere its sanction than in

the infinite power of Beauty, the source of all joys, absolution

of all crimes, eternal worship of all great souls!

Chapter Four: THE DANGEROUS GAME

I

On the wet pillow, dampened by the dual tears of repentance and forgiveness, the two heads, pallid from pleasure, still seek each other's lips, and these tentative kisses die without meeting. Meanwhile, the shiver of absent flesh passes through the fingertips to the very end, and between the eyes, a barrier, an impenetrable veil, rises where the too-short flight of glances breaks. It's the delightful annihilation that follows overly intense pleasures, the semblance of death that throws us at the threshold of Paradise. It seems that she has never given herself so completely, in a more profound abandonment; that her caresses have never had this desperate acuity; that one has crossed the threshold of a new world of unknown caresses. It was not only the pleasure that possession always brought but a pleasure doubled by the cessation of pain. From all that was suffered, whether by doubt or some other cause, the immense joy has grown, and the impression of rising higher has come from rising from the depths of an abyss. All that was nothing more than a collapse has risen like a fairy palace, with shadows softer and fresher. The immense contrast between the painful state in which the soul was immersed and the ecstasy from which it emerges crushes us, like an excess of happiness. If jealousy—and this is the most common case—had been the cause of the quarrel, the enjoyment is further exacerbated by an unhealthy impression, the stings of an infamous goad, and it is like the fierce happiness of a miser who has found his treasure. Whatever the case may be, all those who have forgiven have gone through this fierce ecstasy of a moment when the faculties of physically loving are undeniably multiplied. I have heard many women say that it is good to get angry sometimes, for the infinite joys of reconciliation, and I even know some who intentionally provoke quarrels for the pleasure of the subsequent closeness.

An unfortunate method in love, and one whose dangers I want to highlight here.

II

It is certain that in love, we come to each other with a certain sum of mutual illusions. Let's clarify this point. It is not about illusions regarding the amount of pleasure we will receive from each other. I believe that, in this matter, the dream is often far inferior to reality. The possession of the one we have long desired, whose beauty has subdued all other desires within us, is a happiness of such absolute, perfect essence that everything we could have imagined usually seems to have been nothing. This is because we are the true artisans of our own joy, and the one we attempt to associate with it, in a community of body and soul, is merely the occasion. I've pointed this out before, highlighting the emptiness of jealousy since a stranger cannot truly take anything from our intimate happiness, just as a musician cannot steal Beethoven by playing a piece of his composition on a violin that once belonged to him. What we love is love itself, in a being that provides the motive. Therefore, the illusions I speak of, which must absolutely be preserved, do not pertain to the purely physical role of new connections. There, we are sure to find our satisfaction because we carry it within us, like the wise Bias and his fortune.

What can be illusory is the adaptability of the instrument that surrenders itself to us, the way in which its moral being lends itself to our physical dream. It is the mysterious deepening of nature that will impose its company on us, constituting a fragile and delicate element of happiness and longevity. Well, let's not lean too boldly over the abyss and refrain from trying to decipher the ultimate purpose. Let's be content with being happy with all that beauty gives us and not interrogate Woman too much in the Lover. We would often have reason to regret it.

People can say whatever they want, but there exists an eternal misunderstanding between female souls and ours, and we do not speak the same language—those we love and us. Let's keep our lips for kisses rather than passionate lectures. We would quickly realize that we do not understand each other. This is what should cure us, as from something useless, of any temptation to dispute. Conscience, after all, is merely the ability to consider certain facts as permissible and certain others as forbidden. It is on the very nature of these facts that women usually differ in conception from us.

Ah, that much-desired happiness, which seemed to you more than life, conquered through all the submissions of your soul, through all the lost respects of your thoughts, through the abandonment of all your other joys, through immense melancholies and infinite patience—if you only knew how fragile it is at its core. It is very likely to crumble the day when, recalling the sum of your sacrifices, you have the strange fancy to wonder if the being they aimed at was morally worthy! Avoid that day; for its deceitful light would bring only an inexorable night into your hearts.

III

Show mercy for the discovered faults every day, incessantly, by not discovering them. Have respect for your dream. Even when it's called Musset, I abhor the man who takes pleasure in tarnishing what he once adored. What a commendable act it is to proclaim, even to oneself, that one has been a dupe! And besides, it's not true. I pity the person who, having possessed the one they loved, even if wrongly (as if one could be wrong to love!), finds that they have been deceived. In what frozen senses was their intoxication made that they did not keep it as a fragrance of the Infinite? The memory of that unforgettable hour, that sacred hour that should make us more forgiving than Christs, forgiving even the adulterer. Jesus' greatest merit was that he had gained nothing from the guilty woman by absolving her. The first kiss from a desired woman should carry the forgiveness of all those she may steal from us. And do not think that I am preaching to you a weak morality. It is never weakness to know how to suffer. Those who bring dignity into love are very close to no longer loving.

And that is the only misfortune we should fear in this life. When a woman comes to you, your wishes finally fulfilled, she is all mystery, a sphinx that attracts you as much as a Beauty that charms you. Let her remain like that for you, as long as possible. Can you imagine ever reaching the depths of her thoughts? No, right? Well then, why lean over, in the painful hope of seeing reflected there a star that your sky does not know? Whoever has never looked into the eyes of a woman who is unaware of the depths of her dream, of which distant constellations she spies on us without us being able to catch her ourselves, has never truly looked into the eyes of a woman. It is terrible and charming. And we live on this anxiety as much as on our happiness.

The lover should be, for us, a guest whom we treat as best we can, whom we try to keep for as long as possible. It is a physical practice that we only reach the true joys that love entails through the custom of each other, through a certain habit of caresses that nothing can replace. "Her mouth was in harmony with mine," said a charming writer. This common measure is not achieved with the first kiss. This is what constancy should teach us, as the most honest refinement in matters of pleasure. You may say that many men love change. Allow me to reply that they are mediocre lovers, people with a short-sighted passion, souls lacking depth. Whoever cannot attach himself to a woman is certainly a poorly endowed male, superficially speaking, a lover of quantity rather than quality.

With this well-established, what encouragement for voluntary condescension in love, which alone allows for lasting connections, those that are paid for by a real current of pleasure! What reason is there to look for faults, to unnecessarily distress ourselves? The time of possession should be nothing like the other and should be free of all coquetry.

But, you might ask, what about the ecstatic joy of reconciliation?

Well, it must be sacrificed! Besides, it's only a word that is sacrificed. And forgiveness is also a word. Let's get to the bottom of things. Is forgiving someone forgetting the offense they committed against you? Not at all! You are not the master of your memory. It is simply committing to not hold them accountable, in the future, for the pain they caused you, to cause them similar pain. Well, even if you are sincere, this magnanimity, at least in love, also represents absolutely nothing. Very unconsciously, against our will, we will take into account the forgiven fault because our tenderness will be diminished accordingly. In that kiss of forgiveness, in that embrace of return, it is not our grudges that leave us, unless we exchange them. After the delightful spasm, the forgetfulness of ourselves, the momentary sleep where all notions were lost, dispersed, we find ourselves face to face with the memory. Whether we want it or not, a stone has fallen from the edifice of our Dream, a thorn has grown in the bush that separates the two roads, all sprinkled with our blood. Frequent and intentional quarrels are a lowering of Love and do not leave it the cruel glory of collapsing with some greatness, leaving behind a great image. We are no longer the lumberjack who fells the giant tree with a hard blow of his axe, but the shameful insect that gnaws at the bark and brings leprosy where the foliage once flourished.

Therefore, lovers for whom I write, I owed you this page of frankness. Be content to love each other with full soul and full mouth without asking for painful surprises from Destiny. Populate the garden of your soul not with delightfully poisonous flowers, but let the roses with a loyal heart and always fragrant lips flourish there!

Chapter Five: Is Jealousy Necessary?

33

I

I have never believed I spoke enough about matters of love—at least not with the seriousness they entail. Yes, often I reproach myself for leaving unanswered letters that present cases of passionate morality, not because the desire to address such questions is any less keen within me. But I know there is an audience that prefers cheerful tales. For readers less enamored with Gallic wit and more inclined towards sentimentality, I still want to continue my short studies, and my past correspondences can freely put to the test an experience that a few more years have made even more respectable. For I am at the stage of life where, if it is no longer permissible to love as much, one can better remember.

> *Beneath destiny's lash, where blood stains impose,*
> *Half the earthly journey, through life's throes.*
> *At the peak of virile years, time bestows,*
> *Pity for Love, as the river of existence flows.*
> *Ascended to heights, soon I'll descend,*
> *Echoing emptiness, in days lived, I'll wend.*
> *To the eternal pyre, my ashes I'll send,*
> *A wandering soul, in night's breath, it'll blend.*
> *Veil falls from eyes, a double horizon fades,*
> *Fate wrapped in sorrow, a gaze that persuades.*
> *Far from the cradle, near the tomb's shades,*

Equal road beneath azure, life cascades. And from this melancholic return to the past, the only impression that remains with me is that I have lost all the time I did not give to Love. And from this anxious glance into the future, nothing remains within me except the fear of not loving enough. For the lovers who will come after, I want, at least, to write what my own joys and sorrows have taught me, to show them, on the journey, the flowers they might forget to pick, to pluck the thorns that would undoubtedly tear at their feet. This knowledge is the only legacy left to me by ancient tenderness, along with the treasure of my memories. I can no longer do much with it for myself, and it is a sweet thought that others, happier, for whom the spring of kisses is rising, will benefit from it. It will teach them nothing more than what La Fontaine so well expressed in that one line from Psyche:

Love! Love! Everything else is nothing!

II

"Should one be jealous?" asks, with admirable seriousness, a college escapee.

Beware, young man. You question me on the point of passionate philosophy where I fear thinking differently than my contemporaries the most.

I am not referring, at least, to the juries that commonly make jealousy the excuse for murder. For everything today is an excuse for murder, especially the pleasure one may have taken in committing it. To disagree with the judiciary of my country on this matter would be quite indifferent to me. They understand true morality as much as I do the drafting of encyclicals. No, it is not the opinion of the legal professionals that worries me. It is that of the far more respectable and interesting group of professional Lovers, my colleagues. So, for them alone, I also ask myself, "Should one be jealous?"

That it is a sentiment inherent to those who originally intended to mock or evade it, that is certain. For there is no more dreadful tearing at the heart than the discovery of not being loved. If I see the one whose mouth seems to me the threshold of paradise, tender, in the shadows, her much-desired lips to another, I conceive a terrible pain, that of a collapsing dream, that of a happiness whose ruins crush the heart.

But against whom and against what should one rebel, I ask you?

Against the woman who lied to you? And, aren't you, as much as her and often more than her, the author of your own illusions, the artisan of your hopes suddenly desperate? Why did you believe too quickly and without sufficient reason to believe? Moreover, who knows if this native perfidy is not one of the cruelest but most enduring charms of our delightful tormentor in this life?

So, against the one who received the sly and quick caress? It would be absolutely lacking in pride, and besides, perfectly useless to dispute with him a possession he is certainly closer to now than you. Against the inevitability of inconstancy? Ah! If we had to curse all the laws that, far from restraining our passions, sharpen them for pain, existence would be nothing but a continual blasphemy. Nevertheless, if jealousy causes you this terrible torture, I see only one remedy: immediate retreat if you are truly a man; forgiveness, alas! if you are man enough to be cowardly, in any case, the most painful of sacrifices or the most humiliating of self-denials. Murder, never! The one jealousy makes commit is the least excusable of all, as it serves no purpose, not even returning love to the one who commits it.

III

There is no logic to demand from a sentiment that must be killed within oneself so that it does not lead you to kill others. I have seen men jealous of a woman's past, throwing at her face affairs they knew perfectly well when they were smitten by them. I have heard fools call this pinnacle of madness the pinnacle of love! If you have not believed, even for a moment, that love, which you hoped to inspire, has renewed everything in a woman's heart just as the love you felt for her has renewed everything in your own heart, you have no right to speak in the name of love, which is, above all, this sublime renewal, this admirable and constant metamorphosis, this divine fire that continually makes us rise from our own ashes. Jealous of the past? I wonder what that could possibly mean for a man who has retained the virile power to love.

But jealousy of the present, the only acceptable one? I come to a delicate point here. Because we live in a society full of compromises where the ideal purity of unique and eternal bonds is allowed only to a privileged few. Most often, those who meet, thirsting for new tenderness, have their feet and hands, if not their hearts, bound by a thousand entanglements. The truth is that one must love as one can in a world where people do not love as they want. To break everything to heroically throw oneself into each other's arms? It's sublime but often difficult—which would be nothing, as material interests do not count in the lofty revolts of the soul—it's bold, but it's almost always outrageously criminal. The chains you break with delight were attached to other hearts that you tear apart by breaking them. With their rings, you toss living shreds that bleed into the wind. Horrible and absolutely guilty! It is not yourself that you sacrifice. It's others! It's not your pains that you offer as a sacrifice on a new altar, but the pains of beings who loved you, and it's not their fault if you no longer love them! Pour all the blood from your chest if it pleases you at the feet of the idol; it's your right! But not a tear from others. It's a crime. Ah! It may seem harsh to you, young man, that one must love only as one can; and yet, it is the law of the wise and those who truly believe in love. Ask yourself then what becomes of jealousy in these necessary resignations, which may be a perversion of our nature but not a perversion for which we are responsible. Could a better social state bring us back to more dignified customs? We are so far from it that I cannot prejudge, as the degradation of customs seems to be increasing. But let's take them as they are. The husband's pain is very legitimate when he discovers the existence of the lover, very legitimate and very logical. But if he punishes, it is in the name of honor, not in the name of love that does not rise from spilled blood.

IV

And the amusing adventures we see alongside the drama of marital jealousy! There are also lovers who are jealous of husbands. I exclude temperaments that make love a purely hygienic diversion, a health gymnastics like hydrotherapy, and I would even wish that the French Academy, which owes us a small service after several centuries of existence, find a name less noble than Love for these singular lovers. I speak of those who bring to it, above all, an elevated psychic sentiment, and who seek a feeling rather than simple sensations. Well, then? Certainly, the preferred one—the most loved one—is that lover to whom a woman, who has not sworn anything to him and owes him nothing, remains relatively faithful, within the limits of her condition. What is he lacking? What is taken from him? The same woman never giving two identical impressions to two different men—because it is within us, and not in the woman, that the source of the impressions lies, and she only makes them spring forth—this one never steals anything from that one.

Lover or husband, to love as one can, it is a melancholic motto, but the only one suitable for our time. We are the children of a century fallen from the ancient ecstasies where heaven and earth, sea and stars, were taken as witnesses. But the need to love remains there, in our being, violated but not suffocated by the absurdity of social conventions, diverted from its flowery course but not dried up. It is no longer a superb river that flows, reflecting the studded azure, but an obscure source, which disperses into a thousand arms where the image of golden stars still trembles. Although marred by its original splendor, it remains nonetheless the most beautiful thing here below and alone carries within itself the heavenly reflections of the Infinite.

To those who meet with hearts wide open and hands extended, one must say: Love each other! Love each other without knowing what you have been or even what you are! What are you? Unfortunates whose lips are dry and thirsty for kisses, victims of eternal spring. Love each other, even in the semblance of the reproach of your collapsed dream and lost illusions, as in a cruelly protective shadow. Love each other, even having lost the sublime right to be jealous!

Chapter Six: The Various Ways of Being Beautiful.

42

I

Conscientious, as always, in the texts I comment on, in these brief studies, I transcribe in these exact terms the question posed to me, to which I will attempt to respond today. What I despair of reproducing is the subjective scribbling. I recently received, from the author himself, a treatise on graphology, and with perfect sincerity, I try to apply its principles to the writings of the women who honor me with their letters. I have not yet encountered a single one that was not disquieting and did not inspire in me the idea of a tranquil life with the one who had penned it. Like happy nations, enviable women have no history. What peculiar state of mind could prompt my correspondents to consult me on matters where the opinion of a man can only be a curiosity, considering that thinking and feeling, first and foremost, have a gender, and the heart does not speak the same language in men and women? This time, however, it is primarily a masculine opinion that is sought from me, and I offer it with perfect sincerity.

"Is it better for honor—husband or lover, it doesn't matter!—(how right you are, Madame!) and from the perspective of sensual happiness (thanks for so much concern!) to have a woman who is correct in her beauty but conceals under the artifices of her attire—so prevalent, alas! today!—more than one flaw in her physical structure, or an unpleasing woman in appearance, but well-made and generously endowed with the details you take pleasure in describing?"

I understand very well, Madame, the details you speak of, and they are the kind that one settles into an armchair to discuss. What can I say! I have a penchant for plumpness, from this perspective, just as others have a fondness for tallness. You'll allow me to find it less perilous. But how you complicate matters for me, in my firm intention to be truthful with myself, by adding: "I am inevitably interested in the question, one of these two cases being mine."

In which of the two do you find yourself, Madame?—Do you want to bet, with me, that it's the second one, that of women better endowed in body than in face? Otherwise, why speak ill of attire? It's a peculiarity reserved for those who would benefit from appearing completely naked. My compliments! But what if I were mistaken? A woman is rarely modest enough to describe her own figure as displeasing. Do you have beautiful eyes and teeth? Then you exaggerate. One is never absolutely ugly with the sky in their gaze and freshness in their kiss. Besides, someone has found you pleasing—husband or lover, it doesn't matter!—since you wonder about the worth of their lot. True, we live in a time when men are less fastidious in matters of beauty than those of the grand centuries where beautiful courtesans were treated as goddesses. Come now! I still don't know if it's your nose that's too large or your backside too small. Forgive my frankness for its ignorance, if it is in any way hurtful to you.

II

"Nothing is sweeter than a sweet visage," said an old French poet, and I would gladly consent to being his grandson. But another wrote, and I would prefer to be his godson:

"Feminine body so tender,

Polly, soft and precious!"

A crucial point to understand, Madame, and one you cannot overlook, given your personal interest in the matter, is who the man is whose sensual happiness is at stake. Because it depends, above all, on the more or less delicate nature of his senses. An unfortunate chance (we should have the right to choose the date of our birth) made me a contemporary of a world of political beasts for whom I harbor a cordial disdain, especially because they bring no artistic concern to matters of passion—the only interesting things on this earth. Deep down, I infinitely prefer, to these parliamentary animals, ruminants and wild beasts that choose their mates with a far more disinterested freedom. Yes, Madame, I make the humiliating admission, but men today generally lack taste and delicacy in matters of beauty. Above all, they lack that noble enthusiasm which, in superior races, prostrated at the feet of the deified woman the living gold of laurels and the red blood of victories. In that time, which was beautiful, Troy was burned for Helen. Now it's cities that are set ablaze for customs disputes. Admit, with me, that these boors have no right to be overly selective. To a vague need for reproduction, which they share with bacteria while remaining inferior in species, they add a hint of self-esteem that makes them citizens. A woman of any structure, with a face that fools say is pretty, is all they need. I suppose it's not this passionate rabble that you want to ensure happiness for. No! You don't have that modesty, and it's about a man—husband or lover—few as they may be today, namely one with a sincere temperament, true love for women, and a soul, at least unconsciously, of an artist. Only he is worth a moment of your sensual interest. Well, for him, the supreme beauty of the body is more than sufficient compensation for facial irregularities, and his choice, if truly free and enlightened, will never hesitate. The scandalous abuse of clothing has led us to this peculiar state where we only appreciate the head in a woman. But in reality, its importance (anatomy in workshops fixes it at a seventh of the whole) is proportional to the space it occupies. Everything else is susceptible not only to beauty, needless to say, but also to expression. Victor Hugo lyrically said that there were "tragic" bellies. There are also idyllic and sublime ones. I have known legs that were so spiritual one regretted their owners didn't use them for writing. The navel is a melancholic eye like that of the water lily. Each dimple in the buttocks, lower back, and shoulders is carved by an invisible but caressing smile. Everything looks, everything attracts in a woman. Everything is alive. The mysterious allure of the lips is a poem where the spirit rises higher than in the noblest conversations. The splendor of forms does more for the serenity of our minds than the useless music of words and the smoke of thoughts. The woman is truly the only book for those who conceive the destiny of our soul only in love.

Ah, you doubt my sincerity. Well, I have known many men who sought almost complete darkness for their pleasures. But I do not share their taste, which I find offensive to their mistresses. I adore the light that lavishes the beauty of she who rests in my arms upon my eyes. If I had been a king, I would have wanted to found my dynasty in the midst of a fireworks display. But I know that this impatience for the sun, where shade is generally more appreciated, is a natural peculiarity, an amorous atavism in the distant cults of Zoroaster. For those who believe, like cats, that the night is the best time to love—and even cats compensate their ears for what their eyes don't see—the question you pose, Madame, obviously resolves itself. The face, whether beautiful or flawed, disappears, but under touch, the delicious perfection of the body remains. The source of infinite joys and ineffable impressions does not dry up in the darkness. The divine feeling of triumphant forms does not abolish itself in shadow. That is truly where the victory of the woman lies, whose tempting reliefs are neither illusions nor lies. The trembling hand revives all the memories of enchanted eyes, unraveling the rosary of mystical admirations and fervent caresses. Sublime joys of blind Homer clinging to the only immortal poem, the Iliad of feminine graces.

III

You see, Madame, my stance is firmly taken. I hope it aligns with serving your romantic interests best. In practice, it is often challenging to adopt because contemporary prudishness does not allow enlightenment on all aspects of the matter. An ugly-faced woman is immediately recognized. But a woman beautiful in body only reveals herself, without exposing, to certain delicate individuals who, at first glance, can undress a woman without touching a hook of her corset or a cord of her petticoats. It's a supreme art, but one that requires long and often expensive experience to acquire. Oh, the price women make you pay for these lessons in things! But let's move on. The moral—there's always one in my precious dissertations—is that one should never condemn a woman based on her face and declare her ugly just because her features are less pleasing. A conscientious researcher, a sincere scholar, an upright judge strives to make her reveal the rest before passing judgment. It's a trial method that is not unpleasant to conduct, a jurisprudence one can delve into without boredom, a way to continue the legacy of Cujas that I recommend to lovers of pleasant surprises. One cannot reproduce the scene of the crime too much. Cultivate, my children, these Pandects!

Chapter Seven: The Good Perjury

49

I

If anything could express how Love is above human affairs, it is its absolute independence from that all-too-human and contingent truth that pertains to facts. It belongs to a higher truth, which is only the expression of its immutable and infinitely superior rights. Odious in all other matters, lies can be sublime in the realm of Love. Justly condemned in all other circumstances of life, perjury can be a duty in matters of the heart.

I am not speaking here of love oaths that sensible and experienced people take for what they are – a naively sincere politeness, nothing more than a courtesy. Since one does not truly love when one does not believe one will love forever, it is only natural to say so. It's even implied, but the folly would be to believe it, and the bad faith to pretend, one day, to have believed it. These are merely language formulas. Yet there is a category of truly pious lies, only within the capacity of elite souls, those that prolong the illusion for those no longer loved, those that spare them any suffering. There are cases where frankness would be a crime, a murder. Tell me, what fact or scruple of conscience takes precedence over this one! When, in an admirable verse, Baudelaire expresses indignation that "honesty" should be mixed with the things of Love, it is that bourgeois honesty that I choose to understand, that stupid honesty that refrains from judging, beyond acts, the consequences they may have. It is, however, degrading the human soul in its free will to deny it this judgment, higher than appearances, inspired by a sovereign conception of what is just or unjust. Do you think all the oaths in the world, before the most august courts, would make me utter the word on which a head depends, even if it were the truth, if I privately judged that the person in question did not deserve death? What one would do for that miserable thing called life, how much more would one not do for that divine thing called Love! Ah, all those who have loved know the respect that its slightest sorrows

50

deserve and how much they must be spared for those who love you! It's a doctrine of humanity, but not a doctrine of cowardice, as some purists dare to say. It is through unheard-of personal sufferings, through abominable sacrifices of one's own joys, that one achieves that strength of falsehood on which the fragile happiness of another soul depends. It takes a lot of courage. Cowards, those who lie thus, come now! Their valiant imposture does not diminish their newfound and genuine tenderness. What does one promise to others when one feels loved? Love, being higher than truth, is even more above falsehood.

I know of no more terrible drama in contemporary history than the intimate drama suffered by a remarkable writer of this time. Blind, he had a devoted companion who made him believe in absolute tenderness. Out of love for the truth, a friend told him that she was deceiving him, and he died from it. Do you know of a more horrifying assassination than that? What a lesson for those who believe they have the right to defend our honor against ourselves!

II

But where perjury becomes an absolute duty is when it concerns a woman's honor.

Let's take the most common case: when a husband asks the lover to swear that he has not insulted him.

You see how cruel and inexorable the situation is. Making the requested oath is evading legitimate anger, incurring suspicion of cowardice. So, I will tell you first: Be man enough and have proven yourself sufficiently so as not to fear this torment, only to fear for those whose bravery may be doubted. That is the essential point. But you run another risk: the man questioning you may know much more than he lets on. He may have evidence and set a trap for you. He may, armed with irrefutable facts, later throw your perjury in your face. And that is truly terrible.

Nevertheless, we must be ready to endure it; there is no hiding it: honor is at stake, the virile honor for which any lie is a stain. But do you believe that this male honor would fare much better having betrayed the most sacred of secrets? Honor, we are taught, and it is true, should be dearer to us than life, but not more than the lives of others. Yes, it is your honor as a man that you sacrifice in this circumstance, but you sacrifice it to the one to whom you would have preferred a hundred times to give your life, and you were not given the choice! Therefore, make the sacrifice worthy of her and worthy of your love. Like the ancient butchers who, in pagan festivals, adorned victims to make them more pleasing to the gods, have elevated your honor so high in everything else that you may, at least, have the bitter and profound joy of casting, with it, at adored feet the best of yourself and the very flowers of your soul!

And I say this in the name of true morality - for there are two, regardless of what the fops who once scorned the naive academic Nisard for venturing this truth from the late La Palisse might say. There is the morality that has, not only the gendarmerie but public esteem, two things I place absolutely on the same level - in second place. But there is the other, the great, the true one, which seeks only the approval or blame of the conscience; the one that touches on facts that neither the assize courts nor even passersby could judge; the one that only admits as elements the profound intimacies of the soul. This one truly has other subtleties, other delicacies. As simple as it is to proclaim that one should always tell the truth, defining the case where it is an absolute duty not to tell it is difficult. But the real superiority of this second morality - the other appearing necessary only to those inclined to murder and to boors - is that it is the only one, fundamentally, that concerns itself with respecting what is called in the law: the rights of third parties. Now, in love, "third parties" play a considerable role. The "third party" in the species is the unfortunate woman who can be lost by a word from her lover. The law certainly doesn't care about her, but the morality I preach does, and it has as its sole axiom, its human and divine ideal at the same time, the constant sacrifice of personal interest, the annihilation of that hateful thing called the self, the deep and absolute self-denial before that great law of Love that elevates us the more we humble ourselves before it. In it lies the true kingdom of heaven, where the first shall be last, and where Des Grieux will pass far ahead of Napoleon because he knew how to love better.

No! Perjury is only an empty word when it comes to a woman's honor.

And if this duty of perjury were well written, not in the codes, but in the practical honor manual that true honest people are much more concerned with, husbands would avoid a ridiculous question because they would know the answer in advance, and the naive would no longer fall for this melodramatic word that only has a shameful meaning when lying for oneself!

III

It is, to be honest, one of the most terrible moments in life when a man who has shaken your hand, whom you often respect and have deceived, openly expresses his doubts, eagerly awaiting a confession on the very pallor of your face. Certainly, this is one of the toughest trials of an irregular life. It is up to you, young men, to await it with convinced firmness and the perfect determination to endure everything, even insults, rather than betray a woman who has given herself to you. For I would readily blame you if I did not know the inevitability of our tenderness, for not choosing a scoundrel or a complaisant person to deceive. There is no shortage of them in the world! But if you have not had the chance to misalliance with someone from the left hand, if it is an upright man that you have tried to dishonestly ridicule, your fault has only one possible excuse: true love capable of all sacrifices.

If you have not truly loved, with all the fervor of your heart, you are mere jesters to have thrown yourselves through the honor of a gentleman. It is even necessary that the woman you have chosen be worthy of this magnificent sacrifice if you want me to absolve you, and even praise you. But even if she were the lowest of the low, your duty would remain absolute, that of denying, not only in front of the husband but in front of the entire world if the world had the impertinence to meddle in your affairs. Ah! You want an absolute point of morality? Well, I am going to provide it for you. A man of honor, in any circumstance whatsoever, never discloses the favors bestowed upon him, even if they come from an ordinary creature who still has the right to personally scorn you, even if she makes the entire rest of the universe happy. These are things that a man of some delicacy never boasts about, whether it's about a girl. The lips that recount it are not worthy of the kiss. The secret of given and received caresses must remain in the deepest modesty of the soul. Lying to the mistress who still loves, perjury to the husband who questions, silence to the crowd that spies: that is the duty, clearly and triply formulated. You may say that the truth hardly finds its place there. What does it matter if Love, which is the only Truth, the only Light, and the only Joy, finds its own!

Chapter Eight: What a Woman Is to the One Who Truly Loves Her

56

I

"Is it for having insinuated, albeit timidly, that our earthly companions were not models of fidelity? I have never thought to reproach them, not finding that man deserves more from them, believing that he does not always deserve the discreet care they take to deceive him. Even if they chose not to take this trouble and not spare him any torture, he would still lack the courage to turn away from a torment that is his life, and he would cowardly present a resigned head to the affront. In a world where the impressions of others are measured by my own impressions, Woman appears to me as the mysterious being who knots and unties destinies, incites heroism or restrains it, hastens punishments, appeases angers, consoles despairs, and plays, in a living form, the implacable and divine role of ancient fate.

I imagine her, like Helen on the ruins of Ilium, one foot on conquered humanity, her forehead in the caress of lights and perfumes, alone, raising before the eternal beauty of things the specter of a beauty superior to all others. In her body lives the powerful rhythm of lines and the delicate law of harmonies; the secret of splendid dominations, where the sacred rights of weakness are affirmed, resides in her mind; her heart is the abyss of mercy and pity where forgiveness awaits our miseries. By her very fragility, she is the image of the Dream we carry within us: a dream of abolished splendors, closed Paradises, glimpsed glorious destinies. She is, in our life, like a heavenly guest whom we must treat as a master.

Sarpejeu, Madam, if all this is contempt, I wonder where admiration and respect begin?"

II

"Is it then that the desire we raise towards woman is an outrage?

If you knew how deep a humility is at the core of this seemingly crude worship, what religious turmoil is behind this sensual fervor, you would not deign to be offended for those you defend it against... at least not against me. Haven't I often and melancholically meditated on the immense disproportion of delights that come to us from women and the little we dare to offer them in return? Her love is made of condescension, and ours of wild audacity. I have proclaimed it a hundred times. Isn't the acknowledgment of my memories, from this perspective, the most eloquent confession? In reality, it is the woman who, by descending towards us, treads the path that we believe we traverse with bleeding feet to ascend to her. The earth bites our heels, and the space that separates us would never be crossed if she herself did not have wings. I sincerely pity the man who lacks this sense of our unworthiness, in whom the domineering respect for beauty does not extinguish, even for a moment, the fevers of the flesh, who does not tremble, as at the threshold of a temple, before the bed where the first kiss awaits him!

He who has not known these delicious terrors, these mortal shames, savored this intimate humiliation in the ecstasy of another being, does not know the most secret and profound joys of Love.

Like a traveler who, having reached the summit of snow-capped peaks, gazes emptily over the gaping immensities without thinking to look at the obscure landscape of the valleys at his feet, he is unaware of the height of his happiness. In what my desperate tenderness for woman has less quintessence, that is, in the very ardor of possession she inspires in me, I find only timid homage, and in vain, I seek contempt."

III

In the bitterness of my disappointments, I have never encountered hatred. I am not of the same blood as Ajax, insulting the gods. To man alone, I have reserved my anger, for all the vile things I have seen in him, and never were they more intense than in the hideous spectacle that my contemporaries inspire in me. Even beyond the mire where his ambition and greed plunge him, even when he suffers through women—often unworthy as they are—it is his cowardice alone that I hold against him, and not the admirable instincts of torture of his tormentor. Far from me the idea of futile revolts. The glory of the sun laughs at the blood-soaked theft of our blasphemies. Thus, Beauty soars far above our complaints and rebellions. Everything is an excuse for the crimes of women, and their weaknesses bear their pardon within them. Not because she does not deserve to be treated as a moral being—such a judgment would be disdainful—but because the rigid morality that accommodates the brutality of our nature is forced to soften for her and to adapt to the delicacies of her temperament and mind. She has the right—and she knows it—to certain unconsciousness, because her mission is both cruel and sweet, and it is to these unconsciousness's, moreover, that we owe most often her kindness. Therefore, it would be great injustice on our part to complain about it. Much has been debated about the weakness of women and the ease of their falls. But not enough has been praised for their admirable faculties of recovery. The fallen man sinks into the mud and disappears. It is the everyday experience, and it is never as abundant, under our eyes, as in those troubled hours when honor floats like a dismasted ship on the abyss and threatens to be nothing more than the name of a thing forever swallowed. But how many fallen women have we seen standing again, purified by some noble sentiment, courtesans turned into loyal wives, unfaithful wives turned into sublime mothers! Nothing is more common, for those who know how to look around, than these magnificent leaps of Woman towards the long-deserted ideal, and these resurrections of the numb soul, this awakening of conscience are, for them, a common spectacle.

In a world where impeccability is not precisely the norm, it seems to me that this alone is enough to constitute a kind of moral superiority. But at the very moment of the greatest degradation, between the scoundrel who perjures himself to be named a deputy and the girl who gives herself for bread, or even jewelry, I have never hesitated for a moment. Especially since what they sell, both of them, is damnably more precious in the case of the latter than the former.

IV

Have I said enough to defend myself from an accusation that a man who has faithfully practiced the profession of lover, a career superior to all others, cannot accept? It truly is not my fault if I have never been able to embrace the Christian conception that portrays Woman as the sister of Man. This was my first stumbling block on the path illuminated by the Faith of our ancestors, lit by the very star that guided the Magi. Due to a strange atavism that irresistibly leads me back to an older tradition, the Greek one, the tradition of paganism where the most perfect blossoming of the human spirit is affirmed, I involuntarily consider Woman as a being of a different essence, whom truly advanced civilizations placed far above man, and whom contemporary barbarisms still shamefully persist in placing below. What I cannot accept is this false fraternity that I find humiliating for our mistresses, this deceptive kinship that would turn Love into a constant incest. But it is precisely my admiration for Woman that makes me reject such notions; it is the Greek pity and not the Muslim disdain. If I have sometimes spoken lightly of my idol, it is in the manner of the Athenians who, to mock their Gods in immortal comedies, were nonetheless assiduous in their sacrifices. I have never thought to deny, in women, the moral being, but I believe their morality to be absolutely different from ours—less human since it very well accommodates causing us suffering, more divine since it partakes in impassive fatalities and rests on a very fate, Beauty, whose power no one avoids. Our notions of honesty, currently making such a beautiful confusion, are, for her, dead letters; but we have never had less reason to be proud of them. For her passionate integrity is often superior to ours because she does not conceive rivalry with any other sentiment. Despicable, no! but certainly formidable, too distant and too high for us to be allowed to judge, made for our ecstatic admirations and not for our useless esteem.

Chapter Nine: ON THE PHYSICAL ASPECT OF LOVE

I

It is mostly in the world that one hears young girls say that a man doesn't need to be handsome to be attractive, and it's a theory that worldly men accept with a modesty that does them honor. I don't have to argue against it when it comes to marriage, that is, an institution where practical considerations play a much larger role today than passion. Those who rush into matrimony with the greatest zeal these days are actors, who have little need for it, and business people who can hardly do without it. For the former, this obsession is a lingering protest against their former bohemian reputation. They are keen to establish, publicly and privately—even at the risk of being cuckolded—that they indeed belong to regular, bourgeois life. Well, they would be wiser to be content with the cross that is now placed on their chest while they are alive, and that is planted in cemeteries on their graves, a dual absolution from secular society and the religious world regarding their profession. As for the latter, they find in marriage a legal, almost honored, means of remaining rich while ruining others, which is the pinnacle of their trade. The admirable separation of property is there to allow them to keep their precious comfort while sowing ruin around them, which is obviously an honest consequence and a moral commentary on "just wedlock," as the Code says. In a profession that combines showmanship and business, that of theater directors, you will find an enthusiasm for marriage twice justified. Rare are those who have the integrity to remain single!

I close this parenthesis on a topic where love too rarely has a say, to simply discuss relationships, legitimate or not, but infinitely more serious, where Love is everything. Note that I don't forbid husbands from being lovers. On the contrary! I just observe that they rarely have the opportunity. In unions where the soul truly holds a place, through its noble aspects, is it wise for a woman to disdain, in a man, the beauty of the face and the vigor of the body? I don't think so, and especially

I don't believe that this disdain can be sincere, no matter how much intelligence and fine education we substitute for the lacking physical appeal.

Let's consider a world for which I write even less than for spouses, but which has the advantage of being sincere to the point of cynicism; we do not find that this disdain is fundamentally present in contemporary women. In appearance only, courtesans may prefer ridiculous bankers to well-built store clerks. These ladies do not neglect the financial requirements of their profession, I agree with you on that. A courtesan who does not get paid would be the shame of her profession. It's so true that Empress Messalina, who thirsted more for vice than love and for ignominy than for kisses, took great care to demand the same salary from passersby as her colleagues, so as not to dishonor the lair of Venus Meretrix. But behind the corpulent patrician, Forain will always show us the robust laborer of the last hour, the one who doesn't sell himself. That one is often a brute and yet represents the ideal in these logically infamous existences. As it was asked one day of one of these scavengers of life why she persisted in staying with a scoundrel who beat her when her own beauty assured her well-mannered lovers and, who knows, perhaps respectful ones, she replied with this sublime word: "But if I love nothing, I am nothing!"

And she was right.

Without wanting to take my lessons from the gutter, I admit that this brutal and resigned concession to an element of often torturous beauty, physical vigor, moves me and seems almost nobler than the indifference I see in a more refined social world, an indifference that I want to believe is a pose for the majority or a consolation for ugliness. But, in the passionate world, which lives only on sincerity, deep intimacy, and reciprocal sensual penetration, I truly don't see what charity and benevolence have to do with it.

In women, as in men, regardless of the perversions education has instilled in them, love should primarily stem from sentiment and adoration of Beauty. Don't you find, like me, that accepted ugliness implies a kind of degradation, a suspicion of very complex pleasures, and above all, drawn from a depravity of the mind? I, for one, stand for the heroic health in these matters upon which the salvation of the ideal and the glory of races depend. I remain ardently in the pagan tradition that placed the external harmony of forms, the beautiful moderation of lines, and the splendor of flesh that carries within itself the light above all, as the very seal of an immortal origin. It is lowering oneself not to seek, in the awareness of one's own defects, the sublime compensation of loving someone more beautiful than oneself.

II

This apparent preference of today's women for maturity solely based on intelligence; their sometimes unfair tolerance for decrepit old age, socially honored nonetheless, might well be imposed on them by our own example. Perhaps they adopt this attitude only to be within our reach and not to humiliate us by appearing too superior.

So, who are the women that almost all lovers seek today? The most beautiful ones? Oh, come on! I mentioned that I'm not talking about marriage, as few men excuse it today using the only argument that justifies it: the impossibility of possessing, other than by marrying, a woman one loves. But in relationships that involve a dual choice, have you noticed that the worship of Beauty, which should be the supreme law of life, doesn't play a significant role? Are the most expensive courtesans also the most gifted in terms of physical beauty? I can show you, whenever you want, admirable women who are starving and abominable creatures dripping with jewels, in luxurious surroundings where their faces make you want to look at the backsides of their footmen. This old guard, which has the disadvantage over Napoleon I's guard of not dying, and in front of which Cambronne would not have settled for just talking, is maintained by the youngest and most elegant members of our circles. Hippolyte no longer repeats the charms of Aricie; he sighs, not like Cambronne, but like Marius, along the ruins. He kisses the foot of these ladies that is not yet in the grave.

But peace to these old women with ivory dentures, straw chignons that donkeys are tempted to graze on. Some of them were beautiful under the reign of Louis-Philippe, and perhaps they just have to stop wearing makeup to be beautiful again. True beauty triumphs through all ages and sometimes seems to take on the immortality of marble with the whiteness of hair. But the debutantes, the ones these gentlemen launch, the celebrities of tomorrow, the glorious ones under construction—look at them a bit! Faces crumpled like old handkerchiefs, upturned noses, wasp waists that I wouldn't undertake to provide a sting for, rogue-like feet and hands, a Yvette Guilbert refrain on painted lips on top of it all. This is enough for protectors, often young and entitled to be much more discerning. No concern for the nobility of types, the imprints of the race, for everything that blends the pride of an ideal with the fever of desire!

While they dress these misshapen dolls expensively, sculptors, painters, and even poets who paint and sculpt in their brains pause, moved and contemplative, before the superb creatures who, like a double Mount Aventine, descend from Montmartre or Belleville, dressed like four pennies but made to revive the august shadow of Phidias. Because you can sense, in the instinctive pride of their walk and under their coarse dress, the vibrant harmony of forms and the powerful pulsation of flesh. The foolish rich people might encounter them sometimes as well, but not one of them will ever exclaim, "There is the mistress I want!"

III

Passionate and contemplative lovers, for whom I usually write, forgive me for this melancholic foray into a world where sincere tenderness, those hidden for happiness, does not bloom. You are the guests of the immortal dream from which I would exile everything that reminds of the ugliness of life. To chase away from you, like a bad air, the sadness of this prose lingering on useless realities, let me tell you, before spring leaves us, a spring song made for you:

In the canvas of life where dreams are spun true,
Under the sky's embrace, painting it anew.
By the water's edge, where willows softly hum,
Morning tears turn to pearls, a symphony begun.
Flowers stir with the whispers of the breeze,
Caresses on foreheads, love's sweet unease.
Hold within, my heart, the universal sway,
Love blossoms now under the sunlit display.
Believe in dreams, though lies they may weave,
Languor of wishes, the heart does grieve.
Brief hour's flight, kisses and oaths entwine,
Into the void, a sweet union divine.
Wait at closed doors, plea for joys untold,
Hands full of roses, hearts full of gold.
Smiles may open the gates of Paradise,
Time to love, where forbidden desire lies.
Flee to shady paths, where lovers stroll,
Hand in hand, a journey of heart and soul.
In the realm of love, all paths align,
Time for one path, for both to entwine.
Enamored beings, seeking in space,
Afflicted by love, an eternal grace.
Spirit of flowers, in the breeze does sigh,

Now's the time to love and willingly die.

Chapter Ten: Passionate Subtleties

I

User

Great King, cease to conquer, or I shall cease to write.

Lovers, cease questioning me, or I shall shatter my pen, an image that has never seemed as terrible to me as those who use it suppose. Breaking a sword, that's understandable. But a pen! Truly noble merit. Ah! the inexhaustible subject where I have already roamed so many side paths, like a field whose end is never reached! Like golden wheat among poppies, it is studded with red wounds, and it is the purest blood from our hearts that makes these purple stars gleam. Like golden wheat, it carries life within itself, and the bread of the soul germinates in painful furrows. It is the plain, fertile in joys and sorrows, where our steps cling mysteriously as if stuck.

Ah! Instead of returning to it again, how I would prefer to tell you about the wonderful spectacle I have before my eyes—mountains stretching to infinity, towards bluish horizons, under the circling flight of large birds of prey. And at my feet, torrents rolling, under the green dust of tamarind trees, their silver water chattering like the full pockets; the mysterious contemplation that descends within me from this distant ride, where clouds are like riders who sometimes stop to plant the whiteness of banners in conquered soil. What eternal renewal nature brings in us! Why is it that we find, like wounded animals, that arrow of love whose sting seems to sharpen there again? The desperate thinker sometimes wonders where he could flee from women. And the infinite unfolds before his dream without finding that dark point of Deliverance where he would find himself alone facing himself, in the austere isolation of his own thoughts. Sweet Orpheus had to follow Eurydice to the threshold of the Underworld.

No matter how far one has gone, so far from the city noise of everyday life, nothing is forgotten until one has forgotten the source of eternal torments and the path that leads there, recognizing, like the little Thumb of the tale, what one has left of oneself. Like the sheep that finds its way at the thorn of bushes. And I don't blame those who abuse the postal facilities where our freedom struggles today to pursue me to the edge of the Pyrenean rivers with questions still touching on matters of Love. In reality, it is not they who bring me back there, but I myself who return there due to an incorrigible habit of my mind. I feel like I'm caught in the act when I think of something else. ***"Quidquid tentabam scribere versus erat,"*** said Ovid of himself. Everything I try to write is only a commentary on what I have already written.

This time, a man presents me with a state of mind to which I can only sympathize fraternally. For it is delicate and painful at the same time, and I can express it no better than in his own words: "It often happens to me," he says, "to court a woman for a long time, but a diligent courtship, and no sooner have I obtained what I thought I wanted than an immediate feeling of aversion succeeds the ardor of my desires."

"Aversion" seems a bit harsh, sir. Let me plead for the feeling of vague gratitude that always deserves the pleasure granted, and which is, I believe, in all natures, somewhat generous. "What I thought I wanted" also seems a risky expression. The least you can do is be sure before asking for it. I am curious to see what the lady would say to you, honestly, after saying, "Well, no, that's definitely not what I wanted." I bet she would slap you, and let me tell you that she would be right.

II

And now, let's chat as good friends. I imagine you're by my side, on this mossy rock from which a wild scent rises, and where you can hear the bell of herds tinkling in the distant pastures. There is a Latin proverb to which I could refer you: *"_Omne animal triste præter gallum vel monacum—gratis fornicantem_"* (added the irreverent malice of our ancestors). I didn't need it to be convinced that you are neither a rooster nor a practicing Carmelite in the exercise of amorous burrows. Neither am I.

Everyone, with these two exceptions, I imagine, has gone through these sudden collapses of a satisfied passion, but not everyone retains the same bitterness as you. Sir, you do not value physical love at its true worth. The moment you have just experienced is worth, on its own, a century of attentions, prayers, all the lost time that you seem to regret, and that is a mistake: for I challenge you to find a more enjoyable occupation. You are really unhappy for having dreamed, hoped, sighed! I tell you, sir, that you are very well paid for your trouble. Because if you couldn't afford it, too bad for you! Allow me to tell you, in fact, that it was mainly your business. Reduced to this simple question of sensual ecstasy, love is what one makes of it through the intensity of ardor one brings to it. The loved one is only the occasion. One can make very bad music on an authentic Stradivarius.

III

Certainly, there is something bitter—especially in youth—to observe this sudden void of the most exalted tenderness. For a moment, one blames oneself for mistaking simple desire for love and being so cruelly deceived about one's own feelings. But maturity comes, along with indulgence, making us less severe about this error whose significance should not be exaggerated. Truly, the only one to be pitied in all this is the one who could believe that she was truly and enduringly adored. Perhaps it's partly her fault. Because not all women know how to give themselves. Many, by wanting to be desired for too long, overshoot the mark and transform the desire they inspired into a kind of obstinacy and impatient rage loaded with future resentments. It is especially in this line of thought that there is a truly psychological moment. Men, dominated by self-love, do not get discouraged but are already contemplating revenge in victory. As for me, who puts no vanity in these matters, I have sometimes simply given up on those holding their wishes too high, grown tired, and closed the door to happiness that came too late. But believe me, you have let the opportune hour pass, one way or another, which only leaves pleasant memories.

From your unfortunate experiences, sir, it simply results that you have not yet truly loved.

Despite the platonically foolish school of good Werther, whose music by Massenet I particularly like, everything preceding the trial you complain about is just the prelude to the immortal book of Love. Those are in the most lamentable madness I know, whose suicides I read about in the newspapers, and who killed themselves in despair before being together. They were not allowed to judge, indeed—and you are the living proof—if what inexorably separated them was really a misfortune. Real love, the love for which one truly has the right to die, is the one whose intoxications have been measured, the one that has so firmly riveted your flesh to other flesh that they cannot be torn apart without opening the heart to the mysterious source through which our blood escapes. This love is slowly made up of all the happiness that absolute possession entails. Each caress is like cement hardening the structure; it grows with each kiss, and its insatiability itself is a pledge of duration. It entwines you with a thousand obscure ties, each tearing of which breaks a fiber—subtle and deeply personal fragrances, contacts with sweetness hitherto unknown, absolute enslavement of all the senses, the delightful tyranny of a being whose being dominates yours. But it is clear, sir, that this is perfectly unknown to you. It is both unfortunate and fortunate for you.

But where you reach perfect comedy is when you ask me, in terms of conclusion, if you should get married. Ask that to Rabelais! Perhaps, if you fear cuckoldry like Panurge, I might personally advise you to wait until you are more sure of yourself in the primordial trial of marriage. In the meantime, let yourself live without wishing to suffer too quickly. Nature is made for these delightful cradlings of thought in vague, undefined impressions, not having immediate action as a consequence. They are better life counselors than we are, the great mountains dozing under their helmet of snow, guardians of eternal serenities, letting the torrents roar at their feet unnecessarily loud, like the noise of battles already distant for us, which your impatience aspires to and from which one returns with more than one wound to the heart!

Chapter Eleven: The Illusion in Love

I

"Confess, she said to me, that you only find faults in me. So why do you continue to see me and profess to love me?

And her pretty mouth had ironic curls seeming to part, as if for a bite, revealing the nacre of her teeth.

"You exaggerate immensely, my dear," I replied to her calmly, "in my opinion of you. However, you are less mistaken when speaking of the fidelity of my feelings."

"Admit, though, that if you had known me as I am now for you, you wouldn't have loved me!"

"I apologize, and I would have assumed you worse than, very likely, I would have loved you nonetheless. For its never perfection that I intended to love in you, and I am no longer one of those fools who always imagine, when starting a new love, that they have found it—and who seriously take their sensual itching as a moral tribute to virtue! This naivety is only allowed in extreme youth, in the naive fervors of overflowing health, in the unconscious desire that then pushes us towards all women with easy admiration. It becomes ridiculous in someone who has already lived, who knows well that it's not by speaking of Woman that Plato wrote that the Beautiful is always the splendor of the Good. Thank God! Love has nothing in common with the Academy that awards Montyon prizes. Where would its greatness be if it merged with Logic and only led us to reasonable attachments? It is not an accountant but a poet who imprisons hearts in his often cruel fantasy. He does not wisely pick bouquets in gardens but devastates entire harvests and willingly crowns himself with thorns where our hands have bled. It is to ignore the despotic weight he imposes on our souls to want to give him as a pedestal a bit of that candid snow, so fragile to melt and tarnish, called esteem. Have you ever heard me say anything other than good about my former mistresses? No! Well, do you think I found them more perfect than you? Those who claim to have stopped loving a woman because, in use, they discovered a quantity of flaws never loved her. Everything becomes charming in the being we are truly in love with, or at least, everything is excused to excess, to the point that we might no longer do without it without suffering. Did Socrates separate from Xantippe? And I set aside the unhealthy impression that sometimes comes to us of loving madly one who seems to us the least worthy, with the painful and delicious conscience of our cowardice. Love is, above all, a sublime and foolish need for sacrifice. _**Credo quia absurdum!**_ Saint Paul foolishly said. _**Amo quia absurdum!**_ the true lover can wisely say. What is made to revolt the mind can be made to enchant the heart. Oh, this poorly stifled revolt, this indignation against oneself, this touch of hatred that is at the bottom of truly sensual love—those who have not known them, those who have not relished them with raging satisfaction cannot boast of having loved. I dare not even, while pitying them with a contemptuous pity, condemn those for whom the perfidy of the lover is a love relish, and who draw, from the exasperations of jealousy, a redoubling of shameful and satisfied tenderness of disgrace. It's a morbid phenomenon, the excess of the sense of wild tolerance that is at the bottom of all true love, a lowering of true passion, the forgetting of all dignity, the abdication of the purest nobilities of the soul. But it is, and I know few whom this infamous tickling has not touched!"

II

She had listened to me patiently, quite busy rearranging the frizz of her admirable black hair in the direction she preferred. Then she said calmly, as if summarizing her own aesthetics:

"For me to love, I need illusion."

Ah! How many times have I heard women tell me this nonsense! Illusion, my dear, it's the very denial of love!

Illusion about what? Not about the pleasures it always provides. Because, in love, the first physical experiences are generally spoiled by awkwardness, by shyness, and by a clumsiness that is all the greater the more one is in love—clumsiness that sometimes goes as far as the ridiculous. There is, from the point of view of sensual renewal, a learning process to be done with each other, a delicate learning that must be endured without violence, without discouragement. The divine soul of the violin does not always wake up immediately under the caress of the bow. It's a rhythm to find, a harmony to resolve, the same A to put in... the ear. One can play for a long time before reaching the real and definitive harmony. But once this is achieved, everything becomes progress, and dilettantism develops, and sensual acuity sharpens, and each of the lovers finally discovers in the other, like in an inexhaustible Golconda, treasures foreseen but long jealous of themselves, that magic of caresses that leaves us living only for our living dream. Come talk to us about moral disillusionment in this divine, superhuman, alas! seraphic state of the soul!

Just like love cannot rest on illusion, neither can it rest on esteem.

I imagine, my dear—which is not entirely accurate—that I discover a new virtue in you every day. So, will you tell me a bit about the great merit I have in loving you? The opposite is infinitely more conclusive. One must love, not for this or that reason, but nonetheless, or not get involved at all. But because one loves nonetheless, one is not forced to become foolish. We often speak of the blindness of Love, and we admire ancient wisdom that put a blindfold on it. Despite ancient wisdom, it's nonsense. I don't need to be blind at all to continue loving. I never abdicate the right to judge whom I love, and perhaps my judgment is all the more severe because it is more profound, better based on daily observation. But this judgment does not prevent me from loving. I never believed for a moment that an angel descended from heaven just for me. And that's how one must love to truly love, to love lastingly, not just by contenting oneself with a real error about the person but by visibly facing her as she is, which is painful sometimes but necessary. Where I agree with ancient wisdom is in looking at Love as a fate from which it is impious to want to escape, under which we must bend without rebellion, and infinitely higher than the opinions we can form of each other.

In no case do I believe that men have the right to judge and condemn themselves. It's by a social fiction, perhaps necessary for a society still having a crude ideal of Justice, that we let magistrates delve into souls. It's the instinct of self-preservation, in its most brutally selfish form, that arms the executioner's hand, and justice has nothing to do with this act of defense. But in the passionate order, in love especially, the pretense of judging and condemning is altogether monstrous. Where is our criterion, I ask you? Where is this measure by which consciences will be measured? I can say what in a being revolts or displeases me, but, as that is part of his logic, why should I demand an account of the moderation, the balance even, of his faults and qualities? If he has bound me with that divine chain of shared and deeply felt caresses, if he has enveloped me in the charm where my flesh finds the only joy, if he has given me, in a word, the ineffable, the absolute, the infinite joy of loving, why do I need illusion to continue, in the end, to be happy with the only happiness that is on earth?

III

The Necessary Illusion in Love! Horace, who—without offending the exquisite memory of Lydie—was not, like the two Catulls and like Propertius, one of the great poets of Love, achieved it through a monstrous means, of which he was wrong, for his memory, to boast of the discovery. In the arms of the first courtesan he encountered, he closed his eyes and conjured up the image of the Lover whom he could only possess from afar, through a trick of the mind, through the most debasing of proxies. That, if I'm not mistaken, is the triumph of Illusion. The unfortunate thing is that it is only possible for those who have never truly loved. Can the scent of a certain flesh, a certain kiss, the habit of a certain caress be confused with another aroma, another flavor, another delicacy? Come on! Love is made of the imperious personality of all these things. Its natural exclusivity, when deep and sincere, is made of the possession of these elements found nowhere else but in a certain embrace, on certain lips, in certain familiar poses. And don't think that I render it too purely physical in this way. Such a beauty spot that is ultimately just a delightful little mole, in a certain corner of the cheek or belly, becomes a necessity for us, the _ultima ratio_ of our amorous enchantments. Morally, certain cruelties, the habit of which has become sweet to us, are perhaps no less necessary. And then, the truly charming thing to say to a woman: Madam, I adore you because I enjoy believing you to be entirely different than you really are!

I prefer, more virilely and more honestly, to say to you: My dear soul, I love you as you are, and it's because I love you without harboring any illusions about you that I am sure I love you truly and enduringly.

I noticed that she was asleep, having managed to put her frizz back in the right direction when I finished this speech. But since I had no pretension to convert her, as a woman is, by nature, immutable, like God, I was nonetheless satisfied to have, at least for myself, spoken well according to my feelings.

Chapter Twelve: The Treasure of Morality

82

I

Cursed forever be the useless dreamer
  Who, in his stupidity, first desired
  Embarking on an insoluble and sterile problem,
  To intertwine honesty with matters of love.

Thus speaks Delphine in a remarkable poem by Baudelaire, and those familiar with "Les Femmes damnées" know in what sense Delphine uses the word "honesty." Despite the vehement reproaches the poet directs at her later, she has expressed nothing but sublime naivety. "Honesty" here almost merges with "propriety." Purely physical love has no reason to shy away from its dream. Virgil's motto, *"_trahit sua quemque voluptas_,"* is its rightful motto. Morality truly has nothing to do with it. The truth is that ordinary morality operates in a different realm than love. Does this mean that love has no morality at all? I don't believe so, but it involves a much more delicate and elevated morality, the broad outlines of which I will attempt to define.

If one delves into the essence of things, it becomes apparent that truth is the sole purpose towards which ordinary morality tends. There is, in the final analysis, only one crime: lying, as it is the only one that avoids accountability for punishment. I cannot find a man guilty who accepts, in advance, all the consequences of a freely committed act. Society is immediately armed against him, which is sufficient to render him non-threatening. A man is only guilty of corrupting a girl if he does not marry her afterward, of fathering a child only if he does not raise it. In this world, I find only two things truly detestable: lies and cowardice.

In love, the goal is higher—it is Beauty. Even if it shocks many, I will say that all those who take a woman or a mistress for anything else are immediately, and by that fact alone, outside the law. A woman has the right to be loved for her beauty, and I believe she has no other rights. And let me clarify. She, from this standpoint, is entitled to complete honesty from us. Needless to say, we leave aside, outside of love, fleeting liaisons that serve only the immediate satisfaction of a need. Yet even in these instances, a self-respecting man brings a sense of selectivity, not degrading his pleasure through complete indifference to the one providing it. Without a doubt, these are the only moments in life that contain a touch of the infinite. But I speak of true lovers who come together to give more of themselves to each other.

The first condition of honesty for them is to be guided, in their choice, by a certain physical admiration. Love is, above all, a religion, a worship. Its incense and prayers should be directed only towards an idol worthy of them and not one that mocks them. Everything is advantageous in the pursuit of living Beauty. You may argue that a beautiful mistress exposes you to much more deception. First, this is not true. I have known wonderfully unfaithful women who were not considered beauties. And then, what dignity and pride in the feeling that you exclusively possess a woman because others do not want her? What would you say about a man who abstains from delicious dishes for fear that his cook might keep a piece for himself? I have previously stated my thoughts on jealousy and how its very essence defies analysis. Each person carries within themselves the sum of impressions that constitute their passionate life, and the same woman only develops it in a completely different way for each individual. In this community, no one can claim to have stolen something from another. Nevertheless, jealousy exists, as one of the most blatant proofs of human illogic, as one of the torments that most deeply affects and tears the heart.

But who will speak of the mysterious need for suffering that complicates the delights of love, and if this martyrdom is not often the secret, sometimes shameful, often sublime, of enduring loves? I do not see it, as many overly severe moralists do, as an unclean spur to desire, but as a touching submission to the great natural law that dictates there must always be pain at the heart of pleasure.

O young people, whose age is now only a distant memory for me, young people who, alone, sometimes make me wish to start my life over, renouncing all my experiences for your admirable naivety, choose your mistresses among the most beautiful! Take pride only in everything that constitutes their beauty—the lily-like radiance of their foreheads, the blue or dark flame of their gaze, the sovereign pride of their smiles, their fidelity to the noble feminine types that inspired painting and sculpture. Firstly, you will thus repel your share of responsibility for the corrupting of the race. And secondly, it is on your knees, believe me, that even a woman already possessed must be adored and served. There is no greater and deeper joy than losing oneself in the contemplation of someone more beautiful than oneself, no more intimate delight than absorbing oneself in the mad desire for their ennoblement. Love is a religion before it is morality. But the first point of the latter, which shows us the path to the greatest and most legitimate pleasures, is the pursuit of Beauty, a concern only for economists enamored of repopulation but which must be the constant concern of those who want to be honest lovers. And how this word "honest" grows with this order of consideration! It implies sincerity in expressions of tenderness, which would otherwise seem a humiliating irony. For to tell a woman that you love her is to tell her that you find her beautiful—whether rightly or wrongly—and if truth is not the goal of inquiries in love, it is nevertheless true that one should lie as little as possible. It also implies the duration of the affection to which the soul willingly dedicates itself. Because a woman who has truly been beautiful is always beautiful. She remains beautiful with the natural splendor of her features that age is powerless to distort; she remains beautiful even for the one who possessed her in her youth, with all the magic of memories that are like the oak leaves that winter does not cause to fall but only turns into golden rust.

II

All of this constitutes the morality of love in its early and triumphant stages. The morality of love in its decline is infinitely more meritorious and painful, but it serves as a gentle and necessary safeguard for those who love in their later years. It is another proof of our fragility and powerlessness in the face of happiness when one can cease to desire a woman whom one had chosen for her beauty, and who, as I mentioned earlier, often remains beautiful. Here, we will see how the morality of love differs from the one whose ideal is truth. I know there are those who advise, in such cases, brutal honesty as a duty, and women with doubts often tell us they would prefer it. Beware! If you feel that they still truly love you, be wary of a loyalty that could be deadly.

Some have recently seen on stage a woman who thought it was her dignity to confess to a husband who adored her and asked for nothing, that she had betrayed him, pursuing him with her abominable confession. She was simply a monster. Even if her conscience needed this confession for relief, shouldn't she have prioritized, even her eternal salvation, over the happiness and peace of an innocent being in her crime? Ah, the marvelous probity that sacrifices everything around it to secure moral tranquility for itself! The duty was well defined for this creature, if she truly repented: to humble herself in an unrelenting lie, damn herself if necessary by perjury, to suffer alone for the wrong she had done. How right I was to say that the crime lies solely in evading the painful responsibilities it entails! It wasn't her adultery that was guilty; it was the revelation she made to her husband under the odiously selfish pretext of preserving self-esteem!

Oh, you for whom I write, never obey this cruel honesty. You had the courage to deceive. Have the courage to lie now and maintain your role. Blame yourself for your betrayal! By all means, I have no desire to, convinced that in love, we are never anything but subject to destinies. Do we even have the right to resist the temptations that arise from

Beauty? I, for one, am not convinced, and I leave Saint Anthony his heroism, which I find absolutely ridiculous. But what is beyond doubt is that we do not have the right to inflict suffering on someone who still loves us for our own weaknesses, assuming there is weakness in these legitimate outbursts. It is, I admit, a painful art for certain souls, at least those whose core remains as transparent as clear waters. You will have to learn it, however, when the time comes, you to whom this state of eternal fidelity was not granted. You will have to bear the shame with resigned smiles, and all your moments, all your concerns, will barely be enough for this difficult task of avoiding a ray of light or a tear in the eyes that you will still kiss, with false conviction and deceitful fervor, while closed.

It is another form of the torments of love, and this one carries compensations in the joys—guilty in the eyes of fools only—of delightful and accursed betrayal.

As you can see, there is a morality in love, made up of all the delicacies of the soul. Outside of it, there remains either a past without dignity or a prolific institution. The nobility of the sentiment is judged best in the observance of very high laws, impeccable aesthetics, and refined humanity. In these, we find the real value of men because only those who know how to love truly deserve to be loved!

Chapter Thirteen: Waltzes Without Music

I

I am like the beasts that, lazily stretched at the feet of Orpheus, undoubtedly savored the sweetness of the rhythm far more than the more delicate secrets of the melody, unaware of the charm that comes only from movement enclosed in a cadence. Everything is a dance around us, a mysterious dance conducted by an invisible bow, and we don't even hear the music. To what obscure conductor do the stars obey in their majestic whirl? Does the distant voice of the nightingale rise towards their golden splendor? Apart from the slow evolution that propels the constellations on their ever-unchanging azure path, I swear to you that the stars have tremors that we especially grasp when, upon waking from a dream where the beloved passed, we see her through our tears.

Everything is a waltz in the sovereign sweetness of the starry and falsely motionless heavens, and the intoxication that comes to us is being drawn into this round where subtle, airy arms envelop us in obscure embraces, where golden hair unravels when comets fan out and succumb, carried away into space by mysterious lovers. At our feet, along the shores, the waves also embrace, voluptuously entwined, with flowers of fire in their manes placed by the nocturnal sparkle of the sky. And in the gardens as well, a single breath brings the stems of roses closer, as if toward the stolen kiss taken from the lips of the lost dancer. But it is in the things of the sky that we must blend our souls, where higher breaths teach us eternal tenderness, like the eternal journey of the stars that constant returns bring back to the paths already traversed, which continue and reach each other, no doubt, when the dawn casts the whiteness of a veil between our weary eyes and their fulfilled loves.

Turn, turn, golden stars, on the path to the Infinite!

II

We are in the midst of a spring festival, surrounded by the dazzle of roses and the glory of foliage. But how difficult is happiness for those who have already lived! Who will restore to us the emotion of the first spring that appeared to us, without the mingling of memories of winter? The immense and shadowless joy that made us believe in an eternity of flowers and blue sunshine?

Now, we know which curtain will fall on this apotheosis. In these breezy freshness, we already sense the golden dust with which autumn envelops all things, this dark golden dust rolled by its treacherous warmth. It clings to the greenery, slowly eroding their color, like a deadly kiss that burns the lips where it is received! Under its invisible weight, the stems bow down, and as the sap dries up, the leaves, once open like the pages of a beautiful book, curl up like the hands of little old women, all lined with veins where the blood no longer flows. They also resemble the frozen wings of birds in the immobility of a flight without direction towards the sky. And it is a clattering of tiny skeletons when the wind passes through the branches, an uncountable lament where the irony of dead joys and betrayed hopes sings. It is all the lost rays of the sun that Autumn has woven into a shroud colored with light, a shroud both resplendent and melancholic, made for the sleep of all that was spring glory, splendor, music, and fragrance!

Nevertheless, its breath, laden with showers and storm clouds, stirs and shakes these sonorous debris that collide with a dry rattle of castanets, and suddenly they take flight as if to escape this breath of hurricanes, flying haphazardly, scattered. And it is a grand whirling on the wet velvet of lawns and the crunching sand of avenues, a round with capricious rhythms, a dance of ghosts, meandering following I don't know what fancy captive of itself, with returns and new desperate collisions. These revolts move in a mysterious cycle, and, like those of the constellations, these small pale stars fallen from the tops of oaks and poplars briefly follow the great law of circular gravitations. For, indeed, a sky has descended upon the earth; a firmament has collapsed, the one that still forms above our heads, the verdant vaults from which descend on our foreheads the hospitable serenity of shadow, the caressing coolness of rest.

Turn, turn, dead leaves, on the path to Nothingness!

III

Feeling very small, they puffed themselves up to appear more considerable.

Since they lacked wings at their sides to ascend to the sky of thought, they filled themselves, like balloons, taking advantage of their very emptiness to engulf more smoke. Politics is a gas that performs this double wonder of making human folly majestic, by rounding it, and giving it a superficial flight that amuses the curiosity of onlookers. Thus, they form a people of little bladders, a microcosm of bubbles that sway, as seen on the long sticks of performers at fairs. Fools take them for lanterns and imagine they are enlightened by them. None of these Icaruses of the Louvre will ever be burned by the sun; they can hardly rise higher than the flight of geese, which is sufficient for the crowd to entrust them with saving the distressed Capitols. Only geese, which also fly in flocks, truly cleave the space with their triangular flight and make a real path. They only pretend to move toward a goal; but, in reality, they merely float; they float, while turning, like airy tops, with a rumbling noise that is the music of emptiness. It is in a circle of words, chrysalises of ideas taken flight, that they perform this task of cockchafers. This does not prevent them from holding a considerable place in society, even though the other cockchafers are destroyed there. Honors go straight to them, just as thistles seem to stand up by themselves in front of the rosy noses of donkeys. Their only fault, fundamentally, is mistaking these thistles for palm leaves and believing they graze the soil of Immortality. They take the height of their foreheads for that of their ears. Ah! my cherished little bladders, my dear little balloons. If you only knew how far the firmament where the souls of lovers, artists, and poets soar is from the blue paper ceiling where your modest dreams and panting ambitions stick, waiting to burst like soap bubbles!

Turn, turn, poor ambitious ones, toward the path of Oblivion!

IV

There is only one love in life, but love is often made up of multiple tendernesses.

We are born with an unchanging ideal of Woman, but it usually takes several to embody it. It's like a living fruit that we carry within us, and often, it takes pain to pluck it out, like the child that the woman had in her womb. The tale of Adam's rib doesn't mean anything else. Yes, we are born prisoners of an image, slaves to a type, and we are, in advance, the defeated ones of a certain beauty. All the fatal aspects of Love lie in this secret.

We too struggle within an unyielding circle; we are confined to an invisible world, mysteriously chained to the sphere of a planet by the blind law of our desires.

And we revolve, we revolve around the idol, with litanies of kisses on the lips, chanting the monotonous and sublime hymn of caresses in the vague incense of ecstasies, often falling at the feet of false gods that we later break with anger. Happy is the one who finally encounters the immortal Divinity of his dream; the one in whom the silent aspirations of his earlier thoughts come true; whose forehead is illuminated with his former desires, now turned into happiness, shining brightly like stars! He no longer has the right to complain about having lived, about having suffered; he no longer has to resign himself to the posthumous consolations of a problematic eternity. He had his share, even in this world. For eternity can fit into a minute, through the infinity of joys. Time is an abstraction, a hypothesis, a simple measure of our pleasures or pains. Happy is the one who has found the immortal and unchanging Beloved! It's also a dance that the winged feet of lovers trace on the flowers they do not crush, an endless dance whose music comes from heaven.

Turn, turn, hearts deeply in love, on the sacred path of Love!

Chapter Fourteen: Consolations

94

I

Some, quite cruelly, made me understand that I had outgrown the age to still speak of matters of pleasure and that it is appropriate to leave this subject to those in the full maturity of youth. It might seem naive of me not to share their opinion; however, it is in all sincerity, if not in complete disinterest. I imagine it is not when carried away by the great passionate torrent that leads us up to the age of forty that a man can jot down his impressions of love casually, like tourists in Switzerland. It is then, if not for fools, the time to live and not to write. I admire those who, in this storm, maintain the ability to analyze what they feel and who, in the light of lightning, plunge their pens into their hearts like into an inkwell. This storm may elicit cries of pain from the poet but cannot inspire the meditation of the philosopher. Only when it has passed does a relative silence allow the latter to reflect.

At what point in the preceding period would he do so? Is it at the beginning of his career as a lover, when the senses marvel at every encounter, letting only a shiver reach the heart, a spring made of light tenderness, infinite and passionate eclecticism, wild rushes toward an uncertain ideal floating under brown and blonde locks, shining in black or blue eyes, reborn at every smiling lip, every flesh that stirs caprice, every gaze that implores a caress? But it's a mad dash through kisses and illusions, a flight colliding with all earthly blues, like that of birds, leaving the nest, intoxicated with space and still unaware of the power of their wings. This blind blooming of desire, in all senses, in lost thickets, does not allow us a stopover in the land of wisdom and study. It barely leaves lasting impressions that do not carve into us like the wound of a knife but freeze on the surface only to melt, like ice flowers on windows, in the warmth of the rising sun. And it's not when the time of less risky and deeper tenderness has penetrated us to the marrow of its burns that we feel the strength to expound on our own torments.

The true time to love has come, which leaves us with neither the time nor the desire for anything else. All those images that floated, like dust, in front of the mystery of an immortal type they still concealed, waiting for our souls to mature into irreversible aspirations and great pains, have vanished. Also, the smoke of incense dissipates at the foot of an altar at the time of sacrifice. The Idol is now standing before us, and our knees bend in infinite adorations. But it is not yet the great and religious rest that allows us to exhale these ecstasies in hosannas. It is not on one forehead that the immortal type blooms, nor in one grace, nor in one unique smile. The uncertainties of desire, though more limited, are only more violent, carrying a greater sum of intensity of suffering. It is the time of infidelities full of remorse, jealousies that melt into furious, undeserved pardons, of all the anxieties of passionate life at its peak, fully aware of sovereign pleasures but still drawn into struggles where lovers tear each other apart, like enemies, in battles where they adore each other. It is not here that the rest lies, which a God gives us to sing like Tityre and reason like Melibee.

Nor is it when we are defeated by the definitive charmer, by the siren who, nestled under some nacreous rock, awaited and watched for us in that furious sea, to make us hers in a prison closed only before us by the almighty power of her charms. In this very sweet captivity, it is an infinite languor of our being through a sweetness of complete possession that we had not known until then, through the subtle joy of an abandonment where we keep nothing of ourselves, that the strength to love without mercy comes to us, the crazy desire to gather ourselves and annihilate in a being adorned with greater beauty, whose sight has enslaved our soul. It is not yet to the mind lost in this dream that one should demand axioms and passionate mathematics.

II

But then, can we only speak of love in retrospect, and can the things written about it only be memories, so to speak, from beyond the grave?

I don't believe so because I don't think aging necessarily means ceasing to love. It's just a matter of loving differently. In exquisite verses, André Chénier wished for the tranquility of old age, with young girls caressing white hair. I confess I haven't yet risen to the desire for that platonic joy, and I'm not addressing those who have reached that point. Instead, I speak to those who, still virile, often as much as they ever were, nonetheless do not forget that they have taken the first steps into the decline of life. I would like to tell them, with all sincerity, about the difficult duties that their conscience as lovers entails, as well as the joys still open to them.

Above all, in my opinion, they must renounce "courting," meaning pursuing women who are not visibly inclined towards them, which will be, I agree, increasingly rare but still happens sometimes to men who have not been young for a long time and have every reason to be proud of these spontaneous successes. I mean that a man, assuming he was handsome— an even rarer hypothesis—must be aware that he is no longer, and physically speaking, proposing his conquest is not tempting. Our pride should be never to owe anything, in love, to pity. The more abundantly you have feasted at the table of virile tenderness, the less excusable you are for wanting to gather the crumbs of your own meal. So be an unrelenting bad rich man to yourself and starve rather than beg for alms. I cannot conceive of a man who has reached this degree of debasement accepting that a woman gives herself to him with the suspicion that it is a sacrifice for her. Whoever has known passionate women must disdain being merely tolerated by generous ones. So, do not ask for anything that you are not owed in advance, only what someone wants to give you, and even then, be wary of being merely an object of curiosity and not of tenderness.

I know that people invoke, as a natural law, as the expression of a precarious balance between ages, as a remunerative fact of years, that young girls often willingly give themselves to people of a very mature age and even seem to feel a certain tenderness for them. Anyone with a shred of natural pride will also refuse to take advantage of this blind illusion, to become an accomplice in a real monstrosity, to exploit the uncertainty of the senses in someone imperfectly nubile. Above all, one will not expose oneself to the hatred and revolt that would certainly be directed towards them by someone who, in younger arms and under fresher lips, has finally learned the secret of divine pleasures. Of all the profanations, there is none that angers me more than that of this sacred ignorance, and I know nothing in the Bible, where subjects of horror abound, that repulses me more than that old King David condemning a virgin to the repugnant contact of his senile body to taste a bit of the warmth of her flesh! Ugh!

III

Resolved to no longer court the beauties, as they used to say in old times, and not to take advantage of the innocence of the young, what remains for us, we who Molière dubbed "barbons" from the age of forty, as indicated by characters who lead the first editions of his plays? First and foremost, the one we love with a definitive tenderness, then the friends of the past—if we had the wisdom to remain their friends—and to have many of them, and if absolute fidelity—this rare bird in love—has not yet become beyond our means, which can be somewhat humiliating for the one who is its object, as too complete fidelity can be a backhanded compliment. They, too, have aged, poor things! But a truly touching illusion allows us to see them still as we loved them, through a mirage that aligns with memory. Why wouldn't we have enjoyed, towards them, the same privilege and appear to them as they knew us, or close to it? In any case, the memory they have retained of our ancient gallantries does not permit them to disdain what we are now. Haven't they delightfully contributed to making the ruins that we are? This constancy is not ridiculous and does not constitute a real infidelity to the ideal; it merely reminds us of the path. It is always a sweetness, for those at least who have passed through it without remorse, to relive the life lived, and it is the same very melancholic and sweet feeling that still leads us, as if on pilgrimages, to the places where we suffered, as to those where we were happy. For time does the same very sweet thing to our past joys and sorrows when we awaken them from oblivion! This is because what we call joy and sorrow is always the result of the initial state of our soul, and the same twilight envelops the dawns and sunsets of our thoughts, a last resort for the obstinate of desire: Venus Meretrix, who is not only indulgent to adolescents!

In my humble opinion and in my personal will, this is the dignity in which true lovers should age—proud of the past that defends them against the weaknesses of the future, renouncing even the still-easy victories whose battles are unfair, retaining the lost respect for women within the respect for oneself, the same love for women but discreet, silent, and resigned, hiding it, if necessary, as if it were a crime. For I tell you truly, what can happen worst to a man who has truly had a virile ideal of Love is to become, in his later years, what they call in the provinces, where they are not lacking: "an old pig."

www.ingramcontent.com/pod-product-compliance
Lightning Source LLC
Chambersburg PA
CBHW022030150726

47990CB00002B/898